3/05

CONTINENTS

Europe

Michael and Jane Pelusey

CHELSEA HOUSE
PUBLISHERS
A Haights Cross Communications Company
www.chelseahouse.com

This edition first published in 2005 in the United States of America by Chelsea House Publishers, a subsidiary of Haights Cross Communications.

Chelsea House Publishers
2080 Cabot Blvd West, Suite 201
Langhorne, PA 19047-1813

The Chelsea House world wide web address is www.chelseahouse.com

First published in 2004 by
MACMILLAN EDUCATION AUSTRALIA PTY LTD
627 Chapel Street, South Yarra 3141

Visit our website at www.macmillan.com.au

Associated companies and representatives throughout the world.

Copyright © Michael and Jane Pelusey 2004
Library of Congress Cataloging-in-Publication Data
Pelusey, Michael.
    Europe / by Michael and Jane Pelusey.
    p. cm. – (Continents)
    Includes bibliographical references and index.
    ISBN 0-7910-8279-2
    1. Europe – Juvenile literature. I. Pelusey, Jane. II. Title.
    GB171.P45 2004
    914'.02–dc22

                                                             2004015817

Edited by Angelique Campbell-Muir
Text design by Karen Young
Cover design by Karen Young
Illustrations by Nina Sanadze
Maps by Laurie Whiddon, Map Illustrations

Printed in China

Acknowledgements

The author and the publisher are grateful to the following for permission to reproduce copyright material:

Cover photographs: Geiranger Fiord, courtesy of Photolibrary.com. Red fox, courtesy of Photodisc.

Australian Picture Library/Corbis, p. 9 (top); Corel, pp. 7, 8 (top), 10, 17, 21 (top), 27 (top); Digital Vision, p. 22 (right); Photodisc, pp. 3 (top and center), 13, 15, 22 (left, center), 24, 25 (bottom), 26, 27 (bottom); Photolibrary.com, pp. 9 (bottom), 12 (left), 21 (bottom), 23 (top and bottom), 29; Photolibrary.com/Photo Researchers Inc, pp. 14, 30; Reuters, pp. 3 (bottom), 11, 16, 19, 25 (top), 28; Stockbyte, p. 22 (right).

While every care has been taken to trace and acknowledge copyright, the publisher tenders their apologies for any accidental infringement where copyright has proved untraceable. Where the attempt has been unsuccessful, the publisher welcomes information that would redress the situation.

Please note
At the time of printing, the Internet addresses appearing in this book were correct. Owing to the dynamic nature of the Internet, however, we cannot guarantee that all these addresses will remain correct.

Contents

Glossary words

When a word is printed in **bold**, you can look up its meaning in the Glossary on page 31.

Europe is a continent

Europe is the second smallest continent in the world. Look at a world map or a globe and you can see that the world is made up of water and land. The big areas of land are called continents. There are seven continents:

- Africa
- Antarctica
- Asia
- Australia
- Europe
- North America
- South America.

Borders

The borders of continents follow natural physical features such as coastlines and mountain ranges. Europe's sea borders are the:

- Mediterranean Sea
- Norwegian Sea
- Atlantic Ocean
- Arctic Ocean.

Europe is attached to Asia. Sometimes Europe and Asia are together called Eurasia. The European–Asian border divides Russia and Turkey in two, so both countries are in Europe and Asia. The European–Asian border runs along the:

- Ural Mountains
- Ural River.
- Caspian Sea

World map showing the seven modern-day continents

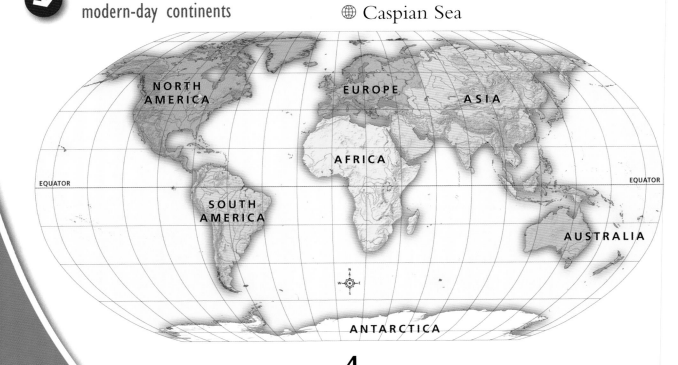

NORTH AMERICA

EUROPE

ASIA

AFRICA

EQUATOR

SOUTH AMERICA

AUSTRALIA

EQUATOR

ANTARCTICA

The world is a jigsaw

The Earth's crust is made up of huge plates, called **tectonic plates**, which fit together like a jigsaw puzzle. These plates are constantly moving, up and down and sideways, up to 4 inches (10 centimeters) a year. Over long periods of time, the plates change in size and shape as their edges push against each other.

Around 250 million years ago, there was one massive supercontinent called Pangaea. Around 200 million years ago, it began splitting and formed two continents. Laurasia was the northern continent and Gondwana was the southern continent. By about 65 million years ago, Laurasia and Gondwana had separated into smaller landmasses that look much like the continents we know today. Laurasia split to form Europe, Asia, and North America. Gondwana split to form South America, Africa, Australia, and Antarctica.

⬆ Europe was once part of the supercontinent Pangaea.

⬆ The European continent formed when Laurasia split into smaller landmasses.

5

Early Europe

When the continents were one, animals moved across the land, since there was no water to stop them. When the continents split apart, the animals were left on separate landmasses and they began to change and develop into the animals we know today. During this time, dinosaurs roamed the Earth, including Europe. As dinosaurs became **extinct**, other animals took over. The first horse, called the hyracotherium, was smaller than a cat and lived on seeds and fruit. Over millions of years, it grew in size and started developing teeth to eat grass. The giant deer lived in Europe between 18,000 and 9,000 years ago.

Early humans

Scientists believe modern humans, or *Homo sapiens*, came from Africa, then made their way to Western Europe around 36,000 years ago. In caves in Southern France, rock paintings have been found that are believed to be over 19,000 years old.

The giant deer had antlers up to 11.5 feet (3.5 meters) wide. ➡

The Parthenon in Athens, Greece

What's in a word?

The word *Europe* comes from the Greek language. *Europa* was a Phoenician princess in Greek **mythology**. In English, *Europa* has become *Europe*.

First civilizations

Early humans in Africa discovered how to grow crops such as wheat and barley. Groups of humans moved together to help each other grow crops and for protection. Eventually, small settlements grew into towns and cities, which became the start of early civilizations.

From Africa, these civilizations spread into southern Europe. They settled along the coast of the Mediterranean Sea and were called Phoenicians.

Early European civilizations

⊕ The ancient Greeks (2,700 years ago) came from the Phoenicians and developed modern ways of running their country.

⊕ The Roman Empire (2,000 years ago) ruled much of Europe. It was the first civilization to build roads and bridges.

⊕ The Vikings (1,200 years ago) came from Sweden, Denmark, and Norway. They were a great seafaring people.

⊕ The **British Empire** (100–200 years ago) sent its navy around the world to discover and **colonize** different countries.

Europe today

St. Peter's Basilica is in the Vatican City.

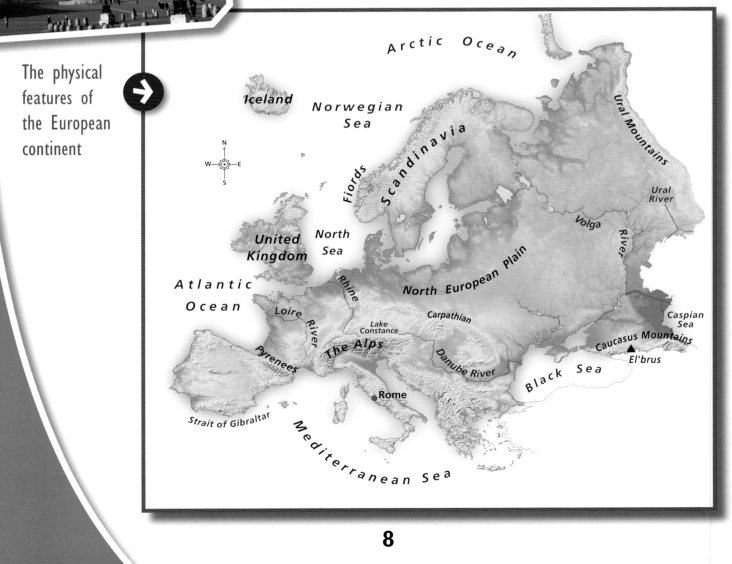

Europe covers an area of 4 million square miles (10.5 million square kilometers). It is made up of 44 countries including Russia and Turkey, which are in both Europe and Asia. The largest European country is Russia at 6.5 million square miles (17 million square kilometers), but only 1.5 million square miles (4 million square kilometers) of that is in Europe. The smallest country in Europe is the Vatican City, which is located in the middle of Rome in Italy. It is only 0.17 square miles (0.4 square kilometers) in size.

The physical features of the European continent

Arctic Ocean

Iceland

Norwegian Sea

Ural Mountains

Scandinavia

Fiords

Ural River

Volga River

United Kingdom

North Sea

North European Plain

Atlantic Ocean

Rhine

Carpathian

Caspian Sea

Loire River

Lake Constance

Caucasus Mountains

Pyrenees

The Alps

Danube River

El'brus

Black Sea

Rome

Strait of Gibraltar

Mediterranean Sea

Physical features

Europe is in the **Northern Hemisphere**, north of the **equator**. The northern part of Europe lies inside the Arctic Circle, which is a land of ice and snow. Europe's northern coastline is made up of steep-sided valleys called fiords. Farther south the land becomes flat. Rivers weave through the flat land, or plains. Between the plains are mountain ranges. In the southern part of Europe, **peninsulas** jut out into the Mediterranean Sea. There are many islands in the Mediterranean Sea and the Atlantic Ocean off Europe. Some islands are part of the European continent, such as the United Kingdom in the Atlantic Ocean.

People

More than 730 million people live in Europe, making it a very crowded continent. European people are made up of more than 150 **ethnic groups** who speak 50 different languages.

The Via Condotti in Rome, Italy, is a busy shopping area.

Geiranger Fiord in Norway is large enough for cruise ships to enter it.

The land

Europe is a land of mountain ranges, islands, and vast **fertile** plains.

Mountains

The highest point in Europe is El'brus, a mountain in the Caucasus Mountains in Russia. It is 18,510 feet (5,642 meters) high. The Urals are the next highest mountain range. There are also three large mountain ranges separating northern Europe from southern Europe. They are the:

- Pyrenees Mountains between France and Spain
- Alps in France, Austria, Switzerland, and Italy
- Carpathians in Eastern Europe.

The highest mountains in Europe outside European Russia are Mount Blanc at 15,770 feet (4,807 meters) and the Matterhorn at 14,777 feet (4,504 meters) high. Both of these mountains are in the Alps.

Plains

North of the Carpathian Mountains lies the fertile North European Plain. Farmers grow crops and graze cattle and sheep on these plains.

The Matterhorn is in the Alps of Switzerland. It is a favorite challenge for many mountain climbers.

10

Rivers

The longest river in Europe is the Volga River, in Russia, at 2,290 miles (3,688 kilometers). Both the Volga and Ural rivers flow into the Caspian Sea. In Western Europe, rivers such as the Rhine, Danube, and Loire are used for transportation and **irrigation** of crops.

Lakes

There are many lakes on Europe's plains. Inland European countries such as Switzerland have no coastline, so lakes provide people with a place to go fishing or boating. One of the biggest lakes in Switzerland is Lake Constance.

Inland seas

The Black Sea and the Caspian Sea are huge seas that are almost completely surrounded by land. Water flows into these seas from big rivers, such as the Danube River that flows into the Black Sea. The Mediterranean Sea and the Atlantic Ocean join together through a small gap between Spain (in Europe) and Morocco (in Africa). This gap is called the Strait of Gibraltar and is only 8 miles (12 kilometers) wide.

Oil rigs in the Caspian Sea in Baku, Azerbaijan

The climate

Europe's climate ranges from cold **arctic** temperatures in the north to hot summers in countries along the Mediterranean Sea.

Arctic

Winter in Northern Europe is very cold. Temperatures in parts of European Russia can drop below −22 degrees Fahrenheit (−30 degrees Celsius). Summers in the north are short and not very warm.

Maritime

Western Europe and the United Kingdom have a **maritime** climate with cool winters and warm summers. Countries with a maritime climate get rain throughout the year and occasional winter snow.

The Gulf Stream
The Gulf Stream in the Atlantic Ocean is a **current** of warm water that flows past Europe. It keeps the climate of Great Britain and western France from getting too cold in winter. Farther inland from the coast, temperatures get much colder in winter and hotter in summer.

 Winter snow covers these streets in Russia.

Climate zones in Europe

KEY
- Mediterranean
- Maritime
- Continental
- Arctic
- Alpine

Continental

Central European countries are surrounded by land, far away from the ocean. They experience a **continental** climate with warm to hot summers and cold winters with snow at times. It rains throughout the year but less often than near the coast.

Alpine

High mountain ranges have their own climate. The Alps and other mountains in Europe get heavy snow in winter and are much colder than the low plains. This is known as an **alpine** climate.

Did you know?
For every 1,000 feet (305 meters) you climb up a mountain the temperature drops 43 degrees Fahrenheit (6 degrees Celsius).

Mediterranean

Countries near the Mediterranean Sea get hot dry summers and mild wet winters. Summer temperatures in Greece, Spain, and Italy can reach 104 degrees Fahrenheit (40 degrees Celsius). Thousands of visitors from Great Britain and Northern Europe spend their summer vacation on beaches around the Mediterranean Sea.

Mountain ranges in Europe have an alpine climate.

Plants and animals

Europe has many different plants and animals. Farms take up much of the land in Europe, which leaves little space for **native** plants and animals. Plants and animals are found mainly in mountainous parts of Europe where farming is more difficult.

Arctic tundra

It gets so cold in the **tundra** that only the top layer of frozen soil thaws out in summer. People cannot grow crops for food in this region. Only small native plants with short roots such as mosses grow there.

In summer, the snow melts enough to uncover these plants. Small animals such as mice come out of **hibernation** to find insects and seeds to eat. Big herds of reindeer feed on the summer plants. Most of the reindeer in the tundra are kept by the Sami people of Scandinavia, who use them for meat and to make leather from their skins.

 Sami men rounding up a herd of reindeer in Lapland

Coniferous forests

Coniferous forests are made up of tall trees that grow seeds in cones. They grow best in cold places such as mountain slopes and northern parts of Europe.

A type of goat called the chamois lives high in the mountains in summer and in the warmer forests in winter.

Deciduous forests

Small patches of oak, birch, and beech trees grow in the warmer parts of Europe. These are deciduous forests, which means the trees drop their leaves before the winter.

Animals that live in deciduous forests include red squirrels, stoats, weasels, badgers, hedgehogs, and wild boars or pigs.

Mediterranean scrubland

Tall trees need lots of water. So, in a Mediterranean climate where there isn't a lot of rain throughout the whole year, trees are more like shrubs. Plants such as rosemary and olive trees grow well in this climate.

Animals that like the warmer weather live in a Mediterranean scrubland environment. Such animals include snakes, lizards, mongooses, lynxes (a type of wildcat), and eagles.

Coniferous forests cloak mountainsides in the French Alps.

The people

Europe is a continent of many people with different beliefs, **traditions**, and languages. They belong to various ethnic groups.

Ethnic groups

Most European countries have their own ethnic group such as the Germans in Germany, French in France, and Swedish in Sweden. Some countries have many

People facts	
Population	730 million people
Most populated country	Russia with 145 million people
Least populated country	Vatican City with 1,000 people
Most crowded country	Monaco with 42,095 people per square mile (16,253 people per square kilometer)

different ethnic groups. Yugoslavia was a country of different ethnic groups such as Croatians, Serbians, and Bosnians. After fighting between these groups in the early 1990s, Yugoslavia was split into five countries to help ease these problems. These countries are now known as:

- ⊕ Yugoslavia (made up of Serbia and Montenegro)
- ⊕ Croatia
- ⊕ Slovenia
- ⊕ Macedonia
- ⊕ Bosnia-Herzegovina.

These women are wearing traditional Croatian dress.

Languages

Europeans speak many languages. Each country has its own language. Two particular European languages, English and Spanish, have spread throughout Europe and the world. English is the third most commonly spoken language in the world. Spanish is the fourth most common language. The Spanish explored both North America and South America. Millions of people from Mexico, Central America, and South America now speak Spanish.

Religion

Europeans follow many religions, the most common being Christianity. There are different forms of Christian religions, such as Catholic, Anglican, Lutheran, and Orthodox. All Christians believe in one God and follow the teachings of Jesus.

Islam is a growing religion in Eastern Europe. People who follow Islam are called Muslims. They also believe in one God and follow the teachings of Muhammad.

 The back of the Catholic Notre Dame Cathedral in Paris, France

The countries

There are 44 European countries, four of which are islands: Ireland, Iceland, Malta, and the United Kingdom.

KEY
- Mediterranean
- Eastern Europe
- Western Europe
- Northern Europe

European regions and countries

United Kingdom in focus

Official name: United Kingdom of Great Britain and Northern Ireland

Area: 94,525 square miles (244,820 square kilometers)

Population: 59 million

Capital: London

Major cities: Liverpool, Manchester, Glasgow, Edinburgh, Cardiff, Belfast

Famous landmarks: Westminster Abbey, Parliament House, and Buckingham Palace in London

Famous people: Queen Elizabeth II

Traditions: cricket, rugby

Traditional food: ploughman's lunch (cheese and bread), steak and kidney pie, cottage pie

The United Kingdom is made up of England, Scotland, and Wales on the island of Great Britain, Northern Ireland, and some small islands.

European power

About 500 years ago, Europeans began sailing around the world looking for new lands to settle. The Spanish, British, Dutch, Portuguese, and French conquered and colonized many new lands. **Descendants** of these Europeans now live throughout North America and South America, Australia, New Zealand, and South Africa. Europeans also ruled and colonized parts of Asia and Africa, but they left when those countries became **independent** during the last 50 years.

European wars

Over thousands of years, European countries have been at war with each other many times. They fought in wars to make their own countries bigger and more powerful. The borders of countries change depending on who wins these wars. In 1945, Germany lost **World War II**. Following World War II, the United States and other troops occupied Western Germany and Russia took over Eastern Germany. The two countries were reunited in 1989.

The Berlin Wall once separated East and West Germany.

Western Europe

There are 11 countries in Western Europe. Use the key below to find out about and compare each country's languages, religions, ethnic groups, agriculture, and natural resources.

Country	Languages	Religions	Ethnic groups	Agriculture	Natural resources
Andorra	Catalan, Dutch, English	Christianity	Andorran, French, Portuguese, Spanish	Cereal grains, Fruit and vegetables, Sheep/cattle/goats	Copper, Iron ore, Lead
Austria	German	Christianity	German	Fruit and vegetables, Sugar beet, Wine, Sheep/cattle/goats	Coal, Oil and gas, Copper, Iron ore, Lead, Salt, Zinc
Belgium	Dutch, French	Christianity	Flemish, Walloon	Sugar beet, Fruit and vegetables, Sheep/cattle/goats, Dairy	Coal, Oil and gas
France	French	Christianity	French, German, Italian	Fruit and vegetables, Sugar beet, Wine, Sheep/cattle/goats, Dairy	Coal, Iron ore, Copper, Zinc
Germany	German	Christianity	German	Fruit and vegetables, Sugar beet, Sheep/cattle/goats	Coal, Iron ore, Copper, Lead, Oil and gas, Zinc
Ireland	English, Gaelic	Christianity	Celtic, English	Fruit and vegetables, Sugar beet, Sheep/cattle/goats, Dairy	Coal, Iron ore, Oil and gas, Lead, Zinc
Liechtenstein	German	Christianity	German	Fruit and vegetables, Sheep/cattle/goats, Dairy	
Luxembourg	French, German, Luxemburgish	Christianity	French, German, Italian	Fruit and vegetables, Wine, Sheep/cattle/goats	
Netherlands	Dutch	Christianity, Islam	Dutch	Fruit and vegetables, Sugar beet, Sheep/cattle/goats, Dairy	Oil and gas
Switzerland	French, German, Italian	Christianity	French, German, Italian	Fruit and vegetables, Sheep/cattle/goats, Dairy	Copper, Iron ore
United Kingdom	English, Gaelic, Welsh	Christianity, Islam	English, Welsh	Fruit and vegetables, Sheep/cattle/goats	Coal, Oil and gas, Copper, Iron ore, Lead, Zinc

Key

Languages
- Catalan
- Dutch
- English
- French
- Gaelic
- German
- Italian
- Luxemburgish
- Portuguese
- Welsh

Religions
- ✝ Christianity
- ☪ Islam

Ethnic groups
- Andorran
- Celtic
- Dutch
- English
- Flemish
- French
- German
- Italian
- Latin
- Portuguese
- Spanish
- Walloon (speak a language similar to French)

Agriculture
- ✤ Cereal grains
- ✪ Dairy
- ✿ Fruit and vegetables
- ☆ Sheep, cattle, and goats
- ☐ Sugar beet
- Wine

Natural resources
- ◆ Coal
- ◆ Copper
- ◆ **Hydropower**
- ◆ Iron ore
- ◆ Lead
- ● Oil and gas
- ◆ Peat
- ◆ Salt
- ◆ Silver
- ◆ Timber
- ◆ Tin
- ◆ Uranium
- ◆ Zinc

France in focus

Official name: French Republic
Area: 211,208 square miles (547,030 square kilometers)
Population: 60 million
Capital: Paris
Major cities: Bordeaux, Marseille, Lyon
Famous landmarks: Eiffel Tower and Arc de Triomphe (an archway) in Paris
Famous people: Brigitte Bardot and Gerard Depardieu (actors), Charles de Gaulle (political leader)
Traditions: petanque (ball game like lawn bowls), wine making
Traditional food: crepes (sweet pancakes), coq au vin (chicken cooked in wine)

France is a large, wealthy country. Paris is the biggest city in Europe. To the east and south are the mountains of the Pyrenees and Central Alps. Rivers such as the Loire and Seine flow though the flat plains where wine grapes are grown.

The Eiffel Tower in Paris

Germany in focus

Official name: Federal Republic of Germany
Area: 137,803 square miles (356,910 square kilometers)
Population: 82 million
Capital: Berlin
Major cities: Frankfurt, Munich, Hamburg, Cologne
Famous landmarks: Brandenburg Gate in Berlin, Rhine and Danube rivers, Black Forest
Famous people: Michael Schumacher (Formula One racing driver), Steffi Graf (tennis player), Ludwig van Beethoven (composer), Albert Einstein (scientist)
Traditions: Bavarian folk dancing, yodeling
Traditional food: wurst (sausages), sauerkraut (pickled cabbage)

Germany has more industry than any other country in Europe. The country has mountains in the south, but the rest of the land is flat and mainly used for farming. The Rhine and Elbe rivers flow north to the ocean.

Neuschwanstein Castle in Southern Germany

Northern Europe

There are nine countries in Northern Europe. Use the key below to find out about and compare each country's languages, religions, ethnic groups, agriculture, and natural resources.

Country	Languages	Religions	Ethnic groups	Agriculture	Natural resources
Denmark (including Greenland)	☐	✝	👤 👤	✤ ❀ ☐ ☆ ✪	◗ ◆
Estonia	☐ ☐ ☐ ☐ ■	✝	👤 👤	❀ ☆ ✪	◗ ◆
Finland	☐ ☐	✝	👤 👤 👤 👤	✤ ☐ ✪	◆ ◆ ◆ ◆ ◆
Iceland	☐ ■ ☐ ☐ ■	✝	👤 👤	❀ ☆	◆ ◆
Latvia	☐ ☐ ☐	✝	👤 👤 👤	✤ ☐ ❀ ☆ ✪	◆ ◆ ◆
Lithuania	☐ ☐	✝	👤 👤	✤ ☐ ❀ ☆ ✪	◆
Norway	☐	✝	👤	✤ ❀ ☆ ✪	◗ ◆ ◆ ◆ ◆ ◆ ◆
European Russia	☐	✝ ☾	👤	✤ ☐ ❀ ☆ ✪	◗ ◆ ◆ ◆
Sweden	☐	✝	👤 👤	✤ ☐ ☆ ✪	◆ ◆ ◆ ◆ ◆ ◆ ◆ ◆ ◆

Key

	Languages	Religions	Ethnic groups	Agriculture	Natural resources
	☐ Danish	✝ Christianity	👤 Celtic	✤ Cereal grains	◆ Coal
	■ English	☾ Islam	👤 Estonian	✪ Dairy	◆ Copper
	☐ Estonian		👤 Finnish	❀ Fruit and vegetables	◆ Geothermal power
	☐ Finnish		👤 Inuit		◆ Hydropower
	■ German		👤 Latvian	☆ Sheep, cattle, and goats	◆ Iron ore
	☐ Icelandic		👤 Lithuanian	☐ Sugar beet	◆ Lead
	☐ Nordic		👤 Norse		◗ Oil and gas
	☐ Norwegian		👤 Norwegian		◆ Peat
	☐ Russian		👤 Russian		◆ Salt
	☐ Swedish		👤 Scandinavian		◆ Silver
	☐ Latvian		👤 Swedish		◆ Timber
	☐ Lithuanian				◆ Uranium
	☐ Ukrainian				◆ Zinc

Sweden in focus

Official name: Kingdom of Sweden

Area: 173,731 square miles
(449,964 square kilometers)

Population: 9 million

Capital: Stockholm

Major cities: Goteburg, Gavle

Famous landmarks: Drottningholm
Palace in Stockholm (home of the
Royal Family), Lake Vanern

Famous people: Greta Garbo (actress),
Alfred Nobel (scientist, founder of the Nobel Prize), Bjorn Borg
(tennis player), ABBA (pop group)

Traditions: smorgasbord (lots of different types of food put out on a table),
Midsummer Evening (the most popular celebration in Sweden)

Traditional food: pickled herring and potatoes, crayfish

Sweden belongs to a group of countries called Scandinavia. Sweden is a
land of many lakes and dense pine forests.

Lake vacation houses are
popular in Sweden.

Russia in focus

Official name: Russian Federation

Area: 6,592,735 square miles
(17,075,200 square kilometers)

Population: 146 million

Capital: Moscow

Major cities: Volgagrad, St. Petersburg, Omsk, Yakutsk

Famous landmarks: Red Square in Moscow,
Volga River

Famous people: Vladimir Lenin, Boris Yeltsin,
Mikhail Gorbachev, and Vladimir Putin (political leaders),
Tchaikovsky (composer)

Traditions: Russian circus, ballet, Russian dolls

Traditional food: caviar (eggs from the sturgeon fish),
borscht (a soup containing beetroot)

Russia is about twice the size of the United States, but
only part of it is in Europe. Most of Russia's people live
in Europe on a big, flat plain. Most crops are grown on
the southern part of the plain, because temperatures
are too cold in the north.

St. Basil's Cathedral in
Red Square, Moscow

Eastern Europe

There are 11 countries in Eastern Europe. Use the key below to find out about and compare each country's languages, religions, ethnic groups, agriculture, and natural resources.

Country	Languages	Religions	Ethnic groups	Agriculture	Natural resources
Belarus	Belarusian, Russian	Christianity, Judaism, Islam	Belarusian, Russian	Cereal grains, Fruit and vegetables, Sugar beet, Sheep cattle and goats, Dairy	Copper, Iron ore, Oil and gas
Bulgaria	Bulgarian	Christianity, Islam	Bulgarian, Russian, Turkish	Cereal grains, Fruit and vegetables, Sugar beet, Sheep cattle and goats, Wine	Coal, Iron ore, Lead, Zinc, Copper
Czech Republic	Czech	Christianity	Czech, Hungarian	Cereal grains, Fruit and vegetables, Sugar beet, Sheep cattle and goats	Iron ore, Copper
Hungary	Hungarian	Christianity	Hungarian	Cereal grains, Fruit and vegetables, Sugar beet, Sheep cattle and goats, Dairy	Iron ore, Oil and gas
Macedonia	Albanian, Macedonian	Christianity, Islam	Macedonian	Cereal grains, Fruit and vegetables, Sheep cattle and goats	Iron ore, Lead, Zinc, Copper
Moldova	Romanian, Russian	Christianity	Moldovan, Russian, Ukrainian	Fruit and vegetables, Cereal grains, Sugar beet, Sheep cattle and goats, Dairy	
Poland	Polish	Christianity	Polish	Fruit and vegetables, Cereal grains, Sheep cattle and goats	Coal, Iron ore, Oil and gas, Copper, Lead, Zinc
Romania	Romanian, Hungarian, German	Christianity	Romanian, Hungarian	Cereal grains, Fruit and vegetables, Sugar beet, Sheep cattle and goats	Oil and gas, Coal, Iron ore, Lead, Zinc, Copper
Slovakia	Slovak, Hungarian	Christianity	Slovak, Hungarian	Fruit and vegetables, Cereal grains, Sugar beet, Sheep cattle and goats	Coal, Iron ore, Copper, Lead
Slovenia	Slovenian	Christianity	Slovene, Hungarian	Fruit and vegetables, Cereal grains, Sugar beet, Sheep cattle and goats	Coal, Iron ore, Lead, Zinc, Silver, Copper
Ukraine	Russian, Ukrainian, Polish, (others)	Christianity	Ukrainian, Russian	Cereal grains, Fruit and vegetables, Sugar beet, Sheep cattle and goats, Dairy	Coal, Iron ore, Oil and gas, Lead, Zinc

Key

	Languages	Religions	Ethnic groups	Agriculture	Natural resources
Key	Albanian Belarusian Bulgarian Czech German Hungarian Macedonian Polish Romanian Russian Slovak Slovenian Ukrainian	✟ Christianity ☾ Islam ✡ Judaism	Belarusian Bulgarian Czech Hungarian Macedonian Moravian Polish Romanian Russian Slovak Slovene Turkish Ukrainian	❖ Cereal grains Dairy ♣ Fruit and vegetables ☆ Sheep, cattle, and goats ▢ Sugar beet Wine	◆ Coal Copper Hydropower ◆ Iron ore ◆ Lead ● Oil and gas ◆ Peat ◆ Salt Silver Timber Uranium ◆ Zinc

Poland in focus

Official name: Republic of Poland

Area: 120,727 square miles (312,683 square kilometers)

Population: 39 million

Capital: Warsaw

Major cities: Gdansk, Krakow

Famous landmarks: Royal Castle and Lazienki Palace in Warsaw, The Tatras (highest part of the Carpathian Mountains)

Famous people: Pope John Paul II (religious leader), Lech Walesa (**democratic** activist and the country's first president)

Traditions: Polish folk art such as paper cutouts and weaving

Traditional food: barszcz (beetroot soup), dill, marjoram, and caraway seeds (spices), wild mushrooms

Most of Poland is made up of low-lying plains with some lakes in the north. Farmers grow crops in the rich soil on these plains. There are some mountains in the south of the country, but they are not very high.

A Polish farmer working his land

Hungary in focus

Official name: Republic of Hungary

Area: 35,919 square miles (93,030 square kilometers)

Population: 10 million

Capital: Budapest

Major cities: Debrecen, Miskolc

Famous landmarks: Lake Balaton, Castle District on the Danube River in Budapest

Famous people: Franz Liszt (composer), Harry Houdini (magician), Johnny Weismuller (Olympic swimmer and actor)

Traditions: folk art such as ceiling and wall painting, pottery, and embroidery

Traditional food: Hungarian goulash (meat and vegetables in a stew), jokai bableves (bean soup)

After World War II, Hungary was ruled by Russia. Later, when the Russian Communist government collapsed, Hungary became an independent country in 1990. The Danube and Tisza rivers flow through Hungary.

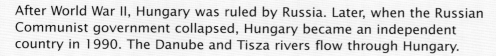

The Danube River flows through Budapest.

Mediterranean

There are 13 countries in the Mediterranean. Use the key below to find out about and compare each country's languages, religions, ethnic groups, agriculture, and natural resources.

Country	Languages	Religions	Ethnic groups	Agriculture	Natural resources
Albania	☐☐	Islam, Christianity	Albanian	Cereal grains, Fruit and vegetables, Sugar beet, Sheep/cattle/goats, Dairy	Oil and gas, Coal, Copper, Hydropower, Iron ore, Zinc
Bosnia–Herzegovina	☐☐☐	Islam, Christianity	Bosniak, Croat, Serb	Cereal grains, Fruit and vegetables, Sheep/cattle/goats	Coal, Iron ore, Copper, Lead, Zinc
Croatia	☐	Christianity	Croat, Serb	Cereal grains, Fruit and vegetables, Sugar beet, Sheep/cattle/goats, Dairy, Olives	Oil and gas, Coal, Hydropower, Iron ore, Zinc
Greece	☐	Christianity	Greek	Cereal grains, Fruit and vegetables, Sugar beet, Sheep/cattle/goats, Dairy, Olives, Wine	Oil and gas
Italy	■	Christianity, Judaism	Italian	Cereal grains, Fruit and vegetables, Sugar beet, Sheep/cattle/goats, Dairy, Olives	Oil and gas, Coal
Malta	☐■	Christianity	Maltese	Cereal grains, Fruit and vegetables, Sheep/cattle/goats, Dairy	Coal
Monaco	■■■	Christianity	French, Italian, Monegasque		
Portugal	■	Christianity	Portuguese	Cereal grains, Fruit and vegetables, Olives, Wine, Sheep/cattle/goats, Dairy	Copper, Coal, Hydropower
San Marino	■	Christianity	Italian	Cereal grains, Fruit and vegetables, Olives, Sheep/cattle/goats, Dairy	
Spain	■■	Christianity	Spanish	Cereal grains, Fruit and vegetables, Olives, Wine, Sugar beet, Sheep/cattle/goats, Dairy	Coal, Copper, Hydropower, Iron ore, Lead, Zinc
European Turkey	☐☐■	Islam	Turkish, Kurdish	Cereal grains, Fruit and vegetables, Olives, Sugar beet, Sheep/cattle/goats, Cotton	Coal, Copper, Iron ore, Zinc
Vatican City	■■	Christianity	Italian		
Yugoslavia (Serbia and Montenegro)	☐	Christianity, Islam	Serb, Albanian	Cereal grains, Fruit and vegetables, Olives, Sheep/cattle/goats	Oil and gas, Coal, Copper, Iron ore, Lead, Zinc

Key

	Languages	Religions	Ethnic groups	Agriculture	Natural resources
	☐ Albanian	✝ Christianity	Albanian	❖ Cereal grains	Coal
	■ Arabic	☪ Islam	Bosniak	◎ Cotton	Copper
	☐ Bosnian	✡ Judaism	Croat	✪ Dairy	Gold
	Catalan		French	♣ Fruit and vegetables	Hydropower
	☐ Croatian		Greek	● Olives	Iron ore
	■ English		Italian	☆ Sheep, cattle, and goats	Lead
	■ French		Kurdish	☐ Sugar beet	Oil and gas
	☐ Greek		Maltese	✾ Wine	Salt
	■ Italian		Monegasque		Timber
	☐ Kurdish		Portuguese		Uranium
	☐ Maltese		Serb		Zinc
	Portuguese		Spanish		
	☐ Serbian		Turkish		
	■ Spanish				
	☐ Turkish				

Italy in focus

Official name: Italian Republic

Area: 116,305 square miles
(301,230 square kilometers)

Population: 56 million

Capital: Rome

Major cities: Naples, Venice, Bologna, Milan, Florence

Famous landmarks: Colosseum and Roman Forum (ancient ruins), St. Mark's Square in Venice, Dolomite Mountains

Famous people: Sophia Loren (actor), Marco Polo (explorer), Leonardo da Vinci (artist and scientist)

Traditions: painting and sculpture, Venetian glass

Traditional food: pasta such as lasagna and spaghetti, risotto (a rice dish), pizza

The Colosseum in Rome is a famous landmark.

Italy is a long peninsula that juts out into the Mediterranean Sea, and includes the two islands of Sicily and Sardinia. Parts of Italy are mountainous. The Alps are on the border between Italy and Switzerland. Two famous volcanoes are found in Italy: Vesuvius and Etna. In A.D. 79, Mount Vesuvius erupted, covering nearly the entire city of Pompeii.

Greece in focus

Official name: Hellenic Republic

Area: 50,942 square miles
(131,940 square kilometers)

Population: 10 million

Capital: Athens

Major cities: Larisa, Iraklion

Famous landmarks: Parthenon and Acropolis (ancient ruins)

Famous people: Aristotle, Plato, and Socrates (philosophers)

Traditions: Greek **philosophy** and mythology

Traditional food: lamb souvlaki, garlic and yogurt dressing, feta cheese, tomatoes, olives

Santorini is one of the many Greek Islands.

Greece includes the Balkan Peninsula in mainland Europe and more than 2,000 islands in the Mediterranean Sea. Most of Greece is covered in mountains, and only a small area is suitable for farming. Many tourists visit Greece to enjoy beaches on the islands in the Mediterranean Sea.

Europe's future

Although a small continent, Europe is still very powerful in the world. Children in Europe are well educated and most people live in apartments and houses in cities. European **organizations** send money and people who are experts in farming and health to less fortunate places in Africa and Asia.

Challenges

Modern machines that manufactured goods were invented in Europe in the 1800s. That time was called **industrialization** and it made Europe very powerful and wealthy.

Waste products from manufacturing can pollute the air and water. Polluted air causes **acid rain**, which kills trees and plants, and the pollution in many European rivers has killed fish stocks. The people of Europe are trying to fix this problem by making new laws to clean up industries. This is a big challenge for the future.

This is the main plant of the Continental Tire factory in Hanover, Germany.

28

The Euro was introduced in 2000.

European Union

In the past, European countries have fought many wars against each other. Now most Western European countries have come together to form the European Union. They have joined to help each other grow as friends and work as a team. They allow member countries to **trade** their goods among themselves. The European Union even has its own money, called the Euro. Some countries such as the United Kingdom prefer not to use the Euro, although they may decide to in the future.

Europe in review

Europe is the second smallest continent.

Area: 4 million square miles (10.5 million square kilometers)

Population: 730 million

First humans in Europe: 36,000 years ago

First civilizations: Phoenicians 3,600 years ago

Other civilizations: Ancient Greeks, Roman Empire, Vikings, British Empire

Countries: 44

Biggest country: Russia

Smallest country: Vatican City

Most crowded country: Monaco

Highest point: El'brus in Russia at 18,510 feet (5,642 meters)

Longest river: Volga River in Russia

Climate zones: arctic, alpine, maritime, continental, Mediterranean

European regions: Western Europe, Northern Europe, Eastern Europe, Mediterranean Europe

Most common languages: English, French, Spanish, German

Web sites

For more information on Europe go to:
http://www.worldatlas.com/webimage/countrys/eu.htm
http://www.visiteurope.com/

Glossary

acid rain rain that mixes with air pollution

alpine a cold, snowy climate in high mountainous regions

arctic extremely cold climate at or near the North Pole

British Empire a time when England ruled over many countries throughout the world

colonize when one country takes over another country

continental a climate of extreme heat and cold, typical of the interior Northern Hemisphere continents

current moving water in oceans or seas

democratic when people elect their political leaders

descendants people from the same family who live at a later time

equator an imaginary line around the middle of the Earth's surface

ethnic groups types of people who share similar heritage

extinct when no more of a particular species of animal or plant are left on the Earth

fertile soil that is good for growing plants

hibernation when animals sleep in caves or underground to survive cold winters

hydropower power made by fast-flowing water

independent when a country governs itself

industrialization when a country starts developing industry

irrigation pumping or moving water to grow crops

maritime coastal climate that is cool and cloudy

mythology traditional stories used to explain natural phenomena and events, such as the creation of the world

native found naturally in a region

Northern Hemisphere the half of the Earth north of the equator

organizations groups of people working together

peninsulas thin pieces of land that are almost completely surrounded by water

philosophy a way of thinking about the mysteries of life

tectonic plates large pieces of the Earth's crust that move slowly, causing earthquakes

trade to buy and sell goods

traditions the way things have been done for many years

tundra vast, level, nearly treeless plains of the Arctic Circle region

waste products anything left over that cannot be used

World War II a war involving many countries, which lasted from 1939 to 1945

Index